Souls of the Lab

Susan Howe

Souls of the Labadie Tract

A NEW DIRECTIONS BOOK

Acknowledgments: See page 127.

Cover and interior design by Erik Rieselbach
Manufactured in the United States of America
New Directions Books are printed on acid-free paper.
First published as New Directions Paperbook in 2007
Published simultaneously in Canada by Penguin Canada Books, Ltd.

Library of Congress Cataloging-in-Publication Data
Howe, Susan, 1937-
Souls of the Labadie tract / Susan Howe.
p. cm.
ISBN 978-0-8112-1718-7 (alk. paper)
I. Title.
PS3558.O893S68 2007
811'.54--dc22

                         2007034255

New Directions Books are published for James Laughlin
by New Directions Publishing Corporation
80 Eighth Avenue, New York 10011

The silk-worm is a remarkeable type of Christ, which when it dies yields us that of which we make such glorious clothing. Christ became a worm for our sakes, and by his death kindled that righteousness with which believers are clothed, and thereby procured that we should be clothed with robes of glory. (Vid. Image 46. See II Sam. 5.23,24; and Ps. 84.6: The valley of mulberry trees.)
—Jonathan Edwards, "Images or Shadows of Divine Things"

The poet makes silk dresses out of worms.
—Wallace Stevens, "Adagia"

Contents

Errand

During his ministry in Northampton, Jonathan Edwards traveled alone on horseback from parish to parish. Boston was a three-day ride east. It was easier to get to Hartford and New Haven. At Greenfield, the Mohawk Trail began its climb westward toward eastern New York (then frontier territory). As an idea occurred to him, he pinned a small piece of paper on his clothing, fixing in his mind an association between the location of the paper and the particular insight. On his return home, he unpinned each slip and wrote down its associated thought according to location. "Extricate all questions from the least confusion by words or ambiguity of words so that the Ideas shall be left naked" he once wrote. Poetry is love for the felt fact stated in sharpest, most agile and detailed lyric terms. Words give clothing to hide our nakedness. I love to imagine this gaunt and solitary traveler covered in scraps, riding through the woods and fields of Massachusetts and Connecticut.

PERSONAL NARRATIVE

An Acount of what was lost by the souldeirs in that axshon at Dearfield:—

	£	s	d
John Allise, A coat,	1	10	00
Samuel Allise, o, gun & stript,			
Richard Biling, A coat,	3	18	
Robard Boltwhood, o, one iacket,		9	
Samuell boltwhood, a coat,	1	00	00
James bridgmon, a coat & gloves,	1	2	
Joseph Catlin, o, gun & stipt,			
Joseph church, coat & jacket,	1	10	
Samuell crofoot, pr shoose,		6	
Nathaniell dickeson, one hat & pair gloves,	2	7	
Samuell dickeson, a coat,		16	
Samuel foot, o, gun & stript,			
Samuel gilit, pr shoose,		6	
John graves, a coat, wascote & belt,	2		
David hoite, o, gun & stript,			
Thomas Hove, a coat,	1	1	
Jonathan ingrem, o, coat iacket & gun,	3		
John Mounticu, coat & neckeclothes,	1	3	
Ebenezer Seldin, coat & gloves,		16	
John smith, one coat & jacket,	1	6	0
Joseph smith, one coat & gloves,	1	8	0
Beniamin waite, o, stript,			
Daniell warner, coat & jacket,	2	3	00
Ebenezer warner, A coat,	3	9	00
Nathaniell Warner, o, A coat, iacket, gun & hat,	3	6	00
Nathaniell white, coat & hat,	1	6	0
Ebenezer wright, one pr new shooes & spurs		9	00
Sum total, [Sic]	33	5	00
More thirty four s,	1	14	
	34	19	00

The slain marked o

On May 17, 1676 the Reverend Hope Atherton and Steven Williams, along with 160 members of a local militia, marched out into nature from Hatfield, Massachusetts, on a botched expedition against neighboring Sqakeag, Nipmunk, Pocumtuck, and Mahican tribes before the land was subdued. I found their narratives in George Sheldon's *A History of Deerfield Massachusetts,* published in 1895 by the Pocumtuck Valley Memorial Association.

Hope Atherton desires this congregation and all people tha
ar of the Lord's dealings with him to praise and give tha
od for a series of remarkable deliverances wrought for him.
ssages of divine providence (being considered together) m
complete temporal salvation. I have passed through the
the Shadow of Death, and both the *rod* and *staff* of God de
e. A particular relation of extreme sufferings that I have
me, & signal escapes that the Lord hath made way for, I
enly, that glory may be given to him for his works that hav
onderful in themselves and marvelous in mine eyes; & will t
e eyes of all whose hearts are prepared to believe what I sl

A sonic grid of homely minutiae fallen away into posterity carries trace filaments. Tumbled syllables are bolts and bullets from the blue.

I vividly remember the sense of energy and change that came over me one midwinter morning when, as the book lay open in sunshine on my work table, I discovered in Hope Atherton's wandering story the authority of a prior life for my own writing voice.

During the 1970s and early 80s I was a poet with no academic affiliation. We moved to Connecticut from Manhattan because my husband's job required that we live in the general area of New Haven. We found a house in Guilford only a five-minute walk from Long Island Sound. This particular landscape, with its granite outcroppings, abandoned quarries, marshes, salt hay meadows, and paths through woods to the center of town, put me in touch with my agrarian ancestors.

David's position provided certain benefits to his family, most importantly, access to Yale's Sterling Library. It was the first time I experienced the joy of possessing a green card that allowed me to enter the stacks of a major collection of books. In the dim light of narrowly spaced overshadowing shelves I felt the spiritual and solitary freedom of an inexorable order only chance creates. Quiet articulates poetry. These Lethean tributaries of lost sentiments and found philosophies had a life-giving effect on the *process* of my writing.

scow aback din

flicker skaeg ne

barge quagg peat

~~sieve catacomb~~

stint chisel sect

In Sterling's sleeping wilderness I felt the telepathic solicitation of innumerable phantoms. The future seemed to lie in this forest of letters, theories, and forgotten actualities. I had a sense of the parallel between our always fragmentary knowledge and the continual progress toward perfect understanding that never withers away. I felt a harmony beyond the confinement of our being merely dross or tin; something chemical almost mystical that, thanks to architectural artifice, these grey and tan steel shelves in their neo-Gothic tower commemorate in semi-darkness, according to Library of Congress classification.

tub epoch too fum alter rude recess emblem sixty key

14

Font-voices summon a reader into visible earshot. Struggles of conscience are taken up as if they are going to be destroyed by previous states of fancy and imagination. Former facts swell into new convictions. Never the warning of ends only the means. More and more I wished to express the critical spirit in its restlessness.

severity whey crayon so distant grain scalp gnat carol

A number of shelved volumes which are tougher have so compressed their congested neighbors that these thinner often spineless pamphlets and serial publications have come to resemble smaller extremities of smallest twigs along Guilford's West Wood Trails during a dry season. Often a damaged edition's semi-decay is the soil in which I thrive. Armed with call numbers, I find my way among scriptural exegeses, ethical homiletics, antiquarian researches, tropes and allegories, totemic animal parents, prophets, and poets. My retrospective excursions follow the principle that ghosts wrapped in appreciative obituaries by committee members, or dedications presented at vanished community field meetings, can be reanimated by appropriation. Always remembering while roving through centuries that, apart from call number coincidence, there is no inherent reason a particular scant relic and curiosity should be in position to be accidentally grasped by a quick-eyed reader in reference to clapping.

Hook intelligence quick dactyl

Bats glance through a wood
Bond between mad and maid

anonymous communities bond and free

Perception crumbles under character
Present past of imminent future

I believed in an American aesthetic of uncertainty that could represent beauty in syllables so scarce and rushed they would appear to expand though they lay half-smothered in local history.

During the 1980s I wanted to transplant words onto paper with soil sticking to their roots—to go to meet a narrative's fate by immediate access to its concrete totality of singular interjections, crucified spellings, abbreviations, irrational apprehensions, collective identities, palavers, kicks, cordials, comforts. I wanted jerky and tedious details to oratorically bloom and bear fruit as if they had been set at liberty or ransomed by angels.

In 1862 Thoreau begins his retrospective essay called "Walking" by declaring: "I wish to speak a word for Nature, for absolute freedom and wildness." He tells us that when he walks or rather saunters out into nature from Concord, Massachusetts, "Hope and the future. . . . [is] not in lawns and cultivated fields, not in towns and cities, but in the impervious and shaking swamps." He enters each swamp as a sacred place, a *sanctum sanctorum*.

Muffled discord from distance
mummy thread undertow slough

I wished to speak a word for libraries as places of freedom and wildness. Often walking alone in the stacks, surrounded by raw material paper afterlife, my spirits were shaken by the great ingathering of titles and languages. This may suggest vampirism because while I like to think I write for the dead, I also take my life as a poet from their lips, their vocalisms, their breath. So many fruits, some looked firm in spring and seemed to be promising, now amassed according to an impervious classification system. One approach to indeterminism might be to risk crossing into rigmarole as fully stated *ars poetica*. Sauntering toward the holy land of poetry I compared the trial of choosing a text to the sifting of wheat, half wild, half saved.

In Deerfield Meadows he found some horses' bones, from which h
got away some sm ll matter; found two rotted beans in yᵉ meadow
where yᵉ indians had thrashed yᵗ beans, & two blew birds' eggs, w
was all yᵉ provision he had till he got home. He got up to Dᵗ tow
plat before dark, Saturday, but yᵉ town was burned before & no in
habitants, so he kept along. His method of travelling was to go
little ways & then lye down to rest, & was wont to fall asleep, but i
yᵉ nᵗ twice he mistook himself when he awoke, & went back agai
till coming to some remarkable places, he was convinced of his mis
take & so turned abᵗ again, & at length he took this method, to la
yᵉ muzzell of his gun towards his course, but losing so much, he wa
discouraged & laid himself down once & again, expecting to dye; bu
after some recruit was encouraged to set forward again, but meetin
wᵗʰ these difficulties he spent yᵉ whole nᵗ in getting to muddy broo
(or, as some call it, bloody brook); here he buried a man's head i
yᵉ path, yᵗ was drawn out of yᵉ grave by some vermin, wᵗʰ clefts c
wood, &c., and upon yᵉ road to H'f'd was (like Samson after th
slaughter of yᵉ Philistines) distressd for want of drink, & many time
ready to faint, yet got no water till he came to Clay Gully, but dive

Hope Atherton is lost in the great world of nature. No steady
progress of saints into grace saying Peace Peace when there is no
peace. Walking is hard labor. Match any twenty-six letters to sounds
of birds and squirrels in his mouth. Whatsoever God has provided to
clothe him with represents Christ in cross cultural clash conscious
phonemic cacophony. Because the providence of God is a wheel
within wheels, he cannot afford to dishonor any typological item
with stark vernacular. Here is print border warfare *in situ*.

rest chondriacal lunacy

velc cello viable toil

quench conch uncannunc

drumm amonoosuck ythian

Each page is both picture and nonsense soliloquy replete with
transgressive nudges. It's a vocalized wilderness format of slippage

and misshapen dream projection. Lots of blank space is essential to acoustically locate each dead center phoneme and allophone tangle somewhere between low comedy and lyric sanctity.

> Prest try to set after grandmother
> revived by and laid down left ly
> little distant each other and fro
> Saw digression hobbling driftwood
> forage two rotted beans &etc.
> Redy to faint slaughter story so
> Gone and signal through deep water
> Mr. Atherton's story Hope Atherton

"P r e s t"—gives the effect of rushing forward into a syntactic chain of associative logic under pressure of arrest. Ready for action in a mind disposed to try but being upset in advance of itself by process of surrender. "In our culture Hope is a name we give women."

> Philology heaped in thin
> hearing

—only a windswept alphabet monument.

> Cries open to the words inside them
> Cries hurled through the woods

If I were to read aloud a passage from a poem of your choice, to an audience of judges in sympathy with surrounding library nature, and they were to experience its lexical inscape as an offshoot of Anglo-American modernism in typographical format, it might be possible to release our great great grandparents, beginning at the greatest distance from a common mouth, eternally belated, some coming home through dark ages, others nearer to early modern, multitudes of them meeting first to constitute certain main branches of etymologies, so all along there are new sources, some running directly contrary to others, and yet all meet at last, clothed in robes of glory, offering maps of languages, some with shining tones.

> *from seaweed said nor repossess rest*
> *scape esaid*

True wildness is like true gold; it will bear the trial of Dewey Decimal.

SOULS OF THE LABADIE TRACT

In 1684, members of a utopian Quietist sect, consisting mainly of Dutch followers of the French separatist Jean de Labadie, left their headquarters at Wieuwerd in the Netherlands in order to spread the new *oeuvre de dieu* while preparing themselves for the coming millennium. They settled in Bohemia Hundred, Cecil County, Maryland, where Pennsylvania, Delaware, and Maryland meet. The 3,750 acre Labadie Tract, consisting of four necks of land, was bordered on the west by Long Creek, on the north by the cart road to Reedy Island, on the east by the Appoquinnimink Path, and on the South by Great Bohemia Creek. They called it New Bohemia.

I found the term "Labadist" in reference to the genealogical research of Wallace Stevens and his wife Elsie Kachel Moll Stevens during the 1940s.

Jean de Labadie. His reach is through language hints; through notes and maps. In the lapse of time the pressure of others. So it's telepathic though who knows why or in what way

Labadists believed in, among other things, the necessity of inner illumination, diligence and contemplative reflection. Marriage was renounced. They held all property in common (including children) and supported themselves by manual labor and commerce.

In 1702, a Swedish pastor recalled his visit to the group in Maryland. "There are also the Apostles, who were on the Labady at Bohemia when I arrived in this country. Their number is now quite small." In 1722, the community dissolved. When Samuel Bownas visited the site in 1727, "these people were all scattered and gone, and nothing of them remained of a religious community in that shape."

In 1795, Dennis Griffith's landmark map of Maryland noted a "lappadee poplar" at the northern extremity of the Labadie Tract. It was the one tree singled out on the entire map of the state.

The wind had seized the tree and ha, and ha,

Wallace Stevens

Indifferent truth and trust
am in you and of you air
utterance blindness of you

That we are come to that
Between us here to know
Things in the perfect way

While I blunder in our blind
world and the public under-
current here grave Nemesis

Greenest green your holy cope
feigned cope and tinsel cap

Green cloud conceals green

valley nothing but green

continually moving then

silk moth fly mulberry tree

Come and come rapture

Poetry you may do the
map of Hell softly one
voice with viol in green
habit or consort twelve

Maniacs and Fantastics
in measured epic dactyl
Far back thinner coranto
one Labadist one Cynic

I'll borrow chapel voices
Song and dance of treble
bass for remembrance Stilt-
Walker Plate-Spinner air
piebaldly dressed heart's
content embroidered note
Distant diapason delight

Chrononhotonthologos

henchman four giants

four skin coats of eyes

Either late or soon

Calling out intervals

One after the other

One *Christographia*
ink not steadfast one
screech-owl feather

Clipped this word—
Strict to its number
The rest come after

Anti-masque of five senses

arms and legs from Alciato

Naked emblemata for pack-

saddle with contiguous *volte-*

face in this sense ownerless

Door of surrender in the old

black letter picture in Alciat

I'd have gone in for you as I

am out and you're forever in

Oh—but of course of course

This sythe alone signifies time

sometimes with its pall pickaxe

paradox a curious little figure

from into the way that leads *to*

Oh—but how would you know

Authorize me and I act

what I am I must remain

only suffer me to tell it

if I can beginning then

Then before—and then

Relict of you predestined
to remain obscure but as
civil lacunae to the least

ramshackle manacle as if
in dark as to lake effect

Now go back to sleep we

can't be crazy the truth is

we couldn't we couldn't

we're the past—we're too

close—to covet—you're

not to be afraid—breathe

Analyze duration as you
wish to the world we are
from this moment forth

quick light clay dust we
dressed today in a hurry

You may amend as you find

The rest are escaped of which

But one escaped in printing

Strife of self this is for flesh

Swim for why not unbelief

To swim for sake of rhyme

for meter faint letter slield

in pencil after subscribeth

Shorthand on it because of

streights all glue for strife

White line of a

hand's breadth

A white wall a

door any place

Millennial hopes

certainly part of it

Labadist theology
Faith its condition
Obedience its sign

Tall clocks some of
them odd and not in
the humbler houses

Great emptiness as
simple as that went
So straight before—

had not been able
then not being idle
went absent away

Now faith is not what we
hereafter have we have a
world resting on nothing

Rest was never more than
abstract since it is empty
reality we cannot escape

Reason throws light open

Who is that phantom in

the foreground after you

Don't be afraid—free as air

Light presupposes open

Distant if a foe not you

Shadowy hush twilight
Mortal piety two doves
three white pigeons wire
artificial bats and owls
Feigned persons pass by
crying out "Oh, Oh—"

Night presently descending
Ample and stately night

To go down the bay or
cross back bridle time
hold fast mere wanton
gilding almost nothing
Thus poems diagrams
crying out "Oh, Oh—"

We are strangers here
on pain of forfeiture

Oh I see—I have to see

you fresh as those rough

streams are as power is

Caught—and wide awake

Oh—we are past saving

Aren't odd books full of us

What do you wake us for

Aren't we the very same
as we long ago saw and
little by little thought of it

Oh partly—not altogether

it isn't as if long ago—No
I mean the secret between
my age or any age—you

We needn't dot any i's
We know what we know
We needn't dot any i's

Frivolity step to and fro
Our cross-laced sandals
you dusty ideate echo

Crossroad two antithetical
crossroads motif of mirror
civilly silver when and if

You you loose ramshackle
extract poem do hold ashes
as history qua history half

Those bones the Indian tall
as tall lucky old man as you
cold chilliness yes yes you

with me here between us—of
our being together even in
english half english too late

I keep you here to keep
your promise all that you
think I've wrought what

I see or do in the twilight
of time but keep forgetting
you keep coming back

Stern wars—each are all
in the night here together
Cloth and choir of slate

Hypothesis doesn't stop
What each thought cost
What barbarous claim

Larceny—you may protest
in time you have the start
on our old idols—Apostate

or some torn pieces of sixth
sense at its most fragile in
range of some others of us

"Here we are"—You can't
hear us without having to be
us knowing everything we

know—you know you can't

Verbal echoes so many ghost
poets I think of you as wild
and fugitive—"Stop awhile"

"On his head an oake growing"
Historical distance Campion's
rule of thumb its prior under-

current here on so-called *Earth*
"in a skin coate of grasse greene
a mantle painted full of trees"

See—I have lost your world
I can't for life of me recall
it might have been for light
comes quickly out of itself

I can't attempt to cross over
step by step forgive forgive

Not so—come closest call

for mortality—yes vizard

None on either side *where*

Empty as ever—yes vizard

Closer or closest naught a

faint no to your telescope

Go on go on assuage what

is not who is that phantom

who fell asleep in Christ at

night about two hours after

the sun setting 1770 out of

the frying pan into the fire

Song to Echo in stilt couplet

I'll thine and mine strophe

Web rosette and winged effigy

Sleep of the Just over against

truth of the Truth near as you

can assume cut from the hard

dark slate of Pin Hill Quarry

Now turn to the other side just

here in the other angle yes yes

we've been dying to show you

When I see bravery I admire
everything I hear she didn't
marry did she move too fast
for you I don't see her as too
little in silence in that silent
other place—owls and honor

apart in the dark range others
She left the sect which split

I am too much your mother

as half daughter your quiet

part to go where the gospel

has not been named if I am

willing to hunt in the wood

after sinners it's only after—

Before you are forever after

The place is full of shields blue
satin robes treble cornets an old
enchantress dull Melancholy in
her blue habit sings a short call

Leap-frogging the Middle Ages
I see you and you see I see you

There it is there it is—you
want the great wicked city
Oh I wouldn't I wouldn't

It's not only that you're not
It's what wills and will not

Longing and envying rest

after a little—garden under

trees but better still likely

to be still more anxious to

get to just daylight all I've

always pushed backward

That's the "Labadie Poplar"

Labadists—New Bohemia

little is otherwise known

Our secret and resolute woe

Carolled to our last adieu

Our message was electric

Will you forget when I forget

that we are come to that

"America in a skin coat

the color of the juice of

mulberries" her fantastic

cap full of eyes will lead

our way as mind or ears

Goodnight goodnight

Errand

For twenty-two years, on his daily two-mile walk from home at 118 Westerly Terrace to his office at 690 Asylum Avenue (built on the site of what had once been the Connecticut Asylum for the Education of Deaf and Dumb Persons) or sometimes on noon-hour breaks in Elizabeth Park (once the estate of railroad magnate and treasurer of the State of Connecticut, Charles N. Pond—a spiritualist with a drinking problem*), Wallace Stevens, a surety claims lawyer and later vice-president of the Hartford Accident and Indemnity Company, observed, meditated, conceived and jotted down ideas and singular perceptions, often on the backs of envelopes and old laundry bills cut into two-by-four-inch scraps he carried in his pocket. At the office, his stenographers, Mrs. Hester Baldwin, and Marguerite Flynn, made transcripts. During night hours and on weekends, he transformed the confusion of these typed up "miscellanies" into poems.

In a letter written January 21, 1946, he told Henry Church: "For myself, the inaccessible jewel is the normal, and all of life, in poetry, is the difficult pursuit of just that. . . . During the last few weeks I have been reading a life of Conrad Weiser, even to the exclusion of Pourrat. Weiser emigrated, possibly in the same vessel, with my own people. He became an Indian interpreter and a local hero in my part of Pennsylvania. It has been like having the past crawl out all over the place. The author has not corrected his spelling. When he speaks of pork he spells it borck. This is pure Pennsylvania German and, while it might bore anyone else to shreds, it has kept me up night after night wild with interest."

Today while out walking I experience ways in which Stevens' late poem "The Course of a Particular" locates, rescues, and delivers what is secret, wild, double, and various in the near-at-hand.

---

* "Pond planned to leave the land as a refuge for inebriates but was persuaded to donate it to the city in memory of his wife Elizabeth."

118 WESTERLY TERRACE

His alter ego *"walked"*—

Henry James

In the house the house is all

house and each of its authors

passing from room to room

Short eclogues as one might

say on tiptoe do not infringe

I want my own house I'm

you and you're the author

You're not all right you're

all otherwise it appears as

if you don't care who you

are—if you count the host

Don't worry I go with the
house your living's where
you walk or have walked

I'd rather read than hurt a
hair of you listen to me

Premeditated twilight this
house a nearest wrapped
bundle of belonging idle

Slip back through grasses
dabble our bare feet in

Poets have imagined you
whoever you are implicit
melody familiar metaphor

bawdy tapestries archaic
pillage love patience the
scales the dogs the boots

Lieutenant-of-the-reserve
voice then scraps of tunes
and the scraping of chairs

Walk under paper lantern
nothing secretarial about
this paper house on paper

He had been in ugly houses

fit for one not fit for another

but escaped over roof-edges

Reading on the sofa now for

one other hour despite more

vicissitudes—roof and roof

Back to the doorway flow
of life's great energy this
analogy holds wreathed-
wristed Arcadian Pan in
hidden scrap of draft ode
Pursuit for its own value
half of what's to be won

A smile not of resurrection

when sun appears to come

forth as bridegroom home

Workaholic state of revery

Destititute of benevolence

Does earth rise—nowadays

I see no passage between

Terrors take hold as water

Did the sun set awhile ago

For a first skyscraper one
second glass tower small
introjected guilt parallel

shadow hand signal over
window frame curtain of
house with smug façade

I address you at random

on the subject of doors

Of dim hearsay old age

exile—Snow in letter-life

for now for half an hour

drift tinsel fill the house

Snow cannot take in all tense
creatures of the earth give me
a name I am making it all up
from the secret foundation of
the smallness of earth I bring
birds and animals to children
coming into the world naked
Now show me anything just

Prepare—dress yourself in
cloak of darkness cover in
sticks and straw the private
poor man you would carry
A little redemption toward
the gothic ledge must have
gone in to come out again

Another saucepan wedged
between candles and cups
Low in self abasement light
passes through linen as if
to offer heaven as if roof
will have no hold against
one hour shred of another

Life in this house-island is

riddled with light a sense of

something last to say first

The tone of an oldest voice

Still one of great multitude

Afternoon at its most glassy

The foyer seems to smile

Who's down there with you
One and the selfsame giant
Sometimes bereft in quietness
he makes me as I meet him
grasp his arm—Going about
the house we enter the shade
of a careworn masterpiece

For a long time I worked
this tallest racketty poem
by light of a single candle
just for fun while it lasted
Now I talk at you to end
of days in tiny affirmative
nods sitting in night attire

Two ages overlap you and
your predecessors—where
they go to where far back
becomes silent and all lie
happy down the brain and
barrier self-surrender for
then all doors are closed

I heard myself as if you

had heard me utopically

before reflection I heard

you outside only inside

sometimes only a word

So in a particular world

as in the spiritual world

Face to the window I had

to know what ought to be

accomplished by predecessors

in the same field of labor

because beauty is what *is*

What is said and what this

it—it in itself insistent *is*

It was the passage I always

used at first fall of dusk so

the thought of it hangs like

a bright lamp in the realm

of spirit where each word is

consent to being or consent

to partial being on its own

Before astronomers and
their optical finite world
roofs take longer to run
across do you notice hills
and mountains through all
ages to the beginning of
extremities to a smallest
parable of mustardseed

Perfectly silhouetted first parents
sensible with soundless trust in
fact could leave us all porcelain
Soiled principalities and powers
come up from the four winds a
little nearer even nearer a chest
in attic opens glory delivered to
departed souls who are so used

For a quiet hour I confronted

other nations typical nations

Their land was typical land

Houses were typical houses

Clothes were typical clothes

and indeed the world was a

typical world this quiet one

Once in this quietest room

Ingrafted though it may be
in a gentle distant empire
hereby made beneficial at
evening where there is no
need for sacrifice as if she
lives in an invisible world
frowning on vacancy she
is signaling a lower realm

God was true everything was

a mother's role in childhood

Someone was in that garden

each knowing the other to be

entirely inasmuch what each

believed or what confessed for

cordial confinement is God's

glory each seed every word

There came another as if she
had cleared the high wall she
could see what she saw from
our dining room an old piano
Sound and stillness astir blue
curtain for cover she said to
rest in the house as if I heard
herself as if she saw just so

I write nothing without

coming nearer—Go your

way as if I never appear

to myself or know what

wide windows are what

Laughter at night while

the agitated house slept

I suppose I had expected
outside shade for as long
as you were there—a best
way to picture it would be
foyer faced inward—this
conviction of your spirit
came home to me as *you*

I began to feel you turned

from me—if only turned

round then why not stay—I

cannot stay quiet as an old

woman why can't you stay

quiet in your corner what

sails do you use for flight

Stay on with me face close
to the glass I haven't the
heart he said and he raised
the latch and went upstairs
I never hear of grief when
the sleeping house is shut
I own vast pile of luggage

I know you saw the child
waving signal at stairhead
Last night the door stood
open—windows were port-
holes letters either traced
or lost—historical fact the
fire on hearth or steam in
a kettle year and year out

FRAGMENT OF THE WEDDING DRESS
OF SARAH PIERPONT EDWARDS

the   past

wing^{oint of}   whose

metam ble

S o u l winte onvi becoming   alker

Snow slant th at lead   it

traced 8 and
        the folder (folded paper) in it has mark
        her white fol
"A Piece of th Jonathan Edwards and th Pierrepont.
Sarah Pierrepon   727.
        is a small gift

character by intellectual sympathy in transcription

side)

confine

what you read

One paper

your

and confined beauty. the little indication that discrete detail

is a small gift card size envelope.

not just our planet is so finite and infinite Pallid distance our

"A Piece of the Wedding Dress of **A Piece of the Wedding Dress of Sarah Pierrepont.** *Sarah*

that. slipping the fragile fragment from its first folder.

Learned societies on four continents signatures of delegates
their written greetings good wishes of contemporaries.

Iconophobia. What could we do? Were other long tables at a distance locking
all shields together like a roof? Remember I am seated on the edge of sowing seed
and its springing.

Concerto for trumpet and bassoon with string orchestra

A bill to Rev. Sir

from Boston, January 26, 1727

for silver buckles, white gloves,

and a lute string

Indians at Stockbridge

many years later to the

written and delivered

notes for part of a sermon

On the verso side are

Founders of the Academy whose lateness we are here to celebrate.
The thousandth meeting. Programs and proceedings. Greetings from the
President, from the American Philosophical Society (founded 1743).
Greetings from the American Academy of Arts and Sciences.
Speeches about the concept of an academy in America. Greetings from the other academy etc.,
the history of such organizations. We are really technicians not scholars.
    Reception.

le space of time into paper. Generation to

un has one referent and oscillano

'n change at an...

ments to...

val...

hen rags salv...

ling it for th...

est pages ruled in

space that

night

e wc

night

space that

ling in it est pages ruled in

val r onser inen rags salvaç

out clothing of pin holes

and evening twilir

fragile   serenity . when   alphabetic   characters   still

light of twighlight s share the approaching sun necessary
carrying traces ⲧⲏⲁⲛ d

phyllirea

tive

ot phyllirea, chanced, 1810 om a wha

We are all clothed with fleece of sheep I keep saying as if I were singing as these words do. Throw a shawl over me so you won't be afraid to sleep. I have already shown that space is God.

Acknowledgments

Thanks to Jonathan Edwards for "Personal Narrative," to Henry James for "The Jolly Corner," to Wallace Stevens for "The Souls of Women at Night," and "The Hand as Being," to Perry Miller for his edition of Jonathan Edwards's *Images or Shadows of Divine Things,* and to Todd K. Bender for *A Concordance to Henry James's The Awkward Age.*

Some of these poems appeared in the following publications: *Ploughshares, Aufgabe 5, Smartish Pace,* and a broadside was produced by *Belladonna* #68 of another version of "118 Westerly Terrace."

"Personal Narrative" was originally written for a presidential panel called *The Sound of Poetry the Poetry of Sound* at the MLA convention 2006. Poems in "Personal Narrative" are taken from Susan Howe's poem "Articulations of Sound Forms in Time," published by Wesleyan University Press in *Singularities,* 1990.

Illustrated excerpts are from *A History of Deerfield Massachusetts: the times when and the people by whom it was settled, unsettled, and resettled: with a special study of the Indian wars in the Connecticut Valley with genealogies,* by George Sheldon, Deerfield, Mass. [Greenfield, Mass.: Press of E. A. Hall & Co], 1895–96.

A recorded edition of "Souls of the Labadie Tract" with David Grubbs on khaen baet khaen jet, VCS3 synthesizer, and computer, was published by Gastr Virgo Music (BMI) administered in Europe by Rough Trade, Ltd., Feb 2007.

Grateful acknowledgment is made to the Beinecke Rare Book and Manuscript Library for use of the image of the fragment of the wedding dress of Sarah Pierpont Edwards, which resides in the Library's Jonathan Edwards Collection, and also to The Library of Congress for use of the detail of the 1794 map of the State of Maryland.

Roger Cosseboom helped in preparing the manuscript for "Fragment of the Wedding Dress of Sarah Pierpont Edwards."